Urdu
for Children: Book Two

(Grades II and III)

Let's Read Urdu
Part Two

Chief Editor and Project Director
Dr Sajida S. Alvi

Coordinators
Farhat Ahmad, Faruq Hassan, and Ashfaq Hussain

Writers
Humaira Ansari, Firdaus Beg, Rashida Mirza, Hamda Saifi, Zahida Murtaza

Illustrator
Rupert Bottenberg

McGill-Queen's University Press
Montreal & Kingston · London · Ithaca

© Holder of the Chair in Urdu Language and Culture, Institute of Islamic Studies, McGill University, 2004
ISBN 0-7735-2764-8

Legal deposit third quarter 2004
Bibliothèque nationale du Québec

Printed in Canada on acid-free paper

This book has been published with the help of funding from the Department of Canadian Heritage, Multiculturalism Programs.

McGill-Queen's University Press acknowledges the support of the Canada Council for the Arts for our publishing program. We also acknowledge the financial support of the Government of Canada through the Book Publishing Industry Development Program (BPIDP) for our publishing activities.

National Library of Canada Cataloguing in Publication

Urdu for children: book two / chief editor & project director, Sajida S. Alvi.
(Canadian Urdu language textbook series)
For grades 2–3.
ISBN 0-7735-2765-6 (Stories and Poems part one)
ISBN 0-7735-2766-4 (Stories and Poems part two)
ISBN 0-7735-2763-x (Let's read Urdu part one)
ISBN 0-7735-2764-8 (Let's read Urdu part two)
ISBN 0-7735-2761-3 (Let's write Urdu part one)
ISBN 0-7735-2762-1 (Let's write Urdu part two)
1. Urdu language – Textbooks for second language learners – English speakers. I. Alvi, Sajida S. (Sajida Sultana), 1941–
II. Series.
PK1973.U745 2004   491.4'3982421   C2004-902666-6

CONTENTS

English Section

The Story Behind This Project
Acknowledgments
Contributors
About This Book

Urdu Section

THE STORY BEHIND THIS PROJECT

The remarkable story of the Urdu Instructional Materials Development Project began in 1986 when I returned to McGill University as the first appointee to the Chair in Urdu Language and Culture after an absence of nine years from the Canadian scene. During the time I had taught at the University of Minnesota (1977–86), the concept of multiculturalism was developing roots and taking concrete shape through Canadian government policies. The government's Heritage Languages Program, under the auspices of the Department of Multiculturalism, began sponsoring the development of instructional materials in a variety of heritage languages. On my return to Canada, Izhar Mirza, then president of the National Federation of Pakistani Canadians, and the late Muinudin Muin, both community leaders and friends, drew my attention to the need to develop proper Urdu language instructional tools for children. Consequently in May 1990, with funding from the Department of Multiculturalism, we held a one-day conference at McGill University, jointly sponsored by the Federation of Pakistani Canadians and the Institute of Islamic Studies. Its purpose was to assess the need to develop instructional materials in Urdu and to look for people to work on this project. A team of writers and coordinators was established. Thus began the arduous work of a group of individuals, divergent in their backgrounds and professional training but united by a deep sense of mission. Undeterred by difficulties of commuting from Montreal and Ottawa, and within Metropolitan Toronto, the Project team worked for long hours on the weekends and holidays for over seven years to produce two sets of books. In the initial stages of the project, I realized that the members of the writing team who joined the enterprise had the invaluable experience of classroom teaching in the public school system but no experience of writing and publishing. This did not discourage us, however. Through their sheer determination, motivation, and willingness to write several drafts of each story until everyone was satisfied, the team of full-time teachers in the Ontario Boards of Education was transformed into a team of proficient creative storywriters and authors. This was a very gratifying experience for me.

In August 1997, the Urdu Instructional Materials Development Project team members and various Boards of Education in Ontario involved in the project celebrated the Silver Jubilee of the multicultural policy of the Government of Canada with the publication of *Urdu for Children: Book One*. This groundbreaking work, which provides instruction in Urdu for children, is comprised of two volumes of texts accompanied by two audiocas-

settes, a workbook, and a teacher's manual. This work was the first of its kind in terms of the quality of its content, its sensitivity to the needs of children between the ages of four to six in the Canadian environment, and its eclectic combination of traditional and whole-language instructional methods.

This publication was seen as a fitting testament to the commitment of the Department of Multiculturalism to producing quality instructional materials for Canadian children through the International Languages Programme. This programme demonstrates that, while the English and French languages represent the linguistic duality of this nation, there is a place for other international languages, including Urdu, in the rich Canadian mosaic. For the Project team, it was also a way of joining in the celebration of the Golden Jubilee of the birth of Pakistan, where Urdu is the official language of a nation of over 140 million people.

The current book in the series, *Urdu for Children: Stories and Poems*, while similar to the first in methodology, is designed to meet the needs of children between the ages of seven to eight and older. The students' level is based on their facility in reading, writing, and speaking the language rather than their chronological age. The scope of the topics is wider than in Book One, and the forty stories and poems (most of them original and some adapted) are more complex and longer, and the original artwork is richer and more varied. More details are given in the section "About This Book." The English-Urdu and Urdu-English vocabulary lists are more comprehensive than for Book One. Two volumes of *Let's Read Urdu* have been added to help children enhance their reading skills. The two-part *Let's Write Urdu* workbook provides practice exercises in writing and reinforces the new vocabulary introduced in the texts. The *Teacher's Manual* is a comprehensive, activities-based guide for teachers and parents and provides detailed lesson plans for each Urdu text. Two carefully recorded CDs accompanying the two volumes of the textbook, ensure standard pronunciation of words and intonations in sentences, and infuse life into the stories. Original music was composed for the poems, with melodies created for children to sing to help memorize the poems. From the inception of this project, we have kept in mind the needs of children as well as the needs of those parents who have some familiarity with the Urdu language and who wish to be involved in helping their children learn the Urdu language.

The *Urdu for Children* Textbook Series was envisioned as a model that could be adapted for other non-European heritage languages, especially for South Asian languages such as Hindi, Bengali, Punjabi and languages of predominantly Muslim regions such as Arabic, Dari, Persian, Pashto and Sindhi. The Project team sincerely hopes that this vision will be realized in the coming years by the next generation of teachers and policy-makers. It would be a small but significant step in furthering the spirit of multiculturalism by promoting pride in the many Canadian cultural identities. The development of proper instructional materials for the Urdu language shows the commitment of Canadians of Indo-Pakistani origin to safeguarding their rich cultural heritage for future generations. There has been a rapid

growth in the South Asian community in Canada, a majority of whom have come from the Indo-Pakistan subcontinent where Urdu/Hindi is used as a lingua franca. In the 1986 census, the number of Canadians of South Asian origin was 266,800;* by 1991, it was 420,295, an increase of 57.5 per cent. In the 1996 census, the number jumped to 670,585, an increase of 59.5 per cent; and in the 2001 census the number has jumped to 963,190, an increase of 43.6 per cent. We hope that *Urdu for Children: Book One* and *Book Two* will help meet the needs of a rapidly increasing younger generation of the Urdu/Hindi-speaking community in Canada, the United States, and Europe.

The Urdu Language Textbook Series is the first step towards helping children develop Urdu linguistic skills so that they can keep the flame of their heritage and culture alive. In today's global village, knowledge of a third language, and particularly a non-European language such as Urdu, can certainly help Canadian children become proud and self-assured adults and a unique asset to Canadian society. Indeed, cultural and linguistic diversity can be a major source of enrichment in any social and political order. Thomas Homer-Dixon's warning that, in the current race for globalisation, languages and cultures are disappearing at an alarming rate is noteworthy. Such languages, he argues, should be protected and preserved because we need cultural and linguistic diversity to help solve our problems and resolve our conflicts, in the same way that we need varied ecosystems.**

Sajida S. Alvi

---

* Pamela M. White & Atul Nanda, "South Asians in Canada," *Canadian Social Trends* (Autumn, 1989): 7–9.

** Thomas Homer-Dixon, "We Need a Forest of Tongues." The *Globe and Mail*, July 7, 2001.

ACKNOWLEDGMENTS

Many institutions and individuals have worked on this project since its inception in 1990. Judy Young, the erstwhile director of the Heritage Languages Programme in the Department of Multiculturalism, ardently supported the project. The Canadian government's generous grant through her department resulted in the inception and completion of *Urdu for Children: Book One* and *Book Two*. Two other major partners in this venture are the former North York Board of Education (now part of the Toronto District School Board) and the Institute of Islamic Studies at McGill University. The North York Board and those involved in the International Languages Programme supported the project's housing, administration, and funding in addition to hosting regular meetings of the Project team members at the administration building. Among many individuals who worked at the North York Board of Education, special thanks go to Barbara Toye, Armando Cristinziano, and Susan Deschamps for their help and advice in the preparation of applications for funding to Ottawa, submission of progress reports, and careful preparation and implementation of the terms of various contracts signed by the Project team members.

The Institute of Islamic Studies has given substantive and material support to this project since my appointment to the endowed Chair in Urdu Language and Culture in 1986. This included secretarial help, bulk photocopying, postage, long-distance telephone calls, etc., as well as enthusiastic support for the book launch upon the completion of *Book One* in the fall of 1998. My frequent travel to Toronto for meetings with the Project team became part of my routine at the Institute. The publication of *Book Two* would not have been possible without the Institute's generous financial support. This timely assistance is gratefully acknowledged.

For the smooth field testing of the materials, our thanks are due to the following Boards of Education: in Metropolitan Toronto, York Region, North York, and Peel Boards, and in Ottawa, the Carleton Board. Special thanks go to these members of the Steering Committee: Irene Blayney (Carleton Board), Dr. Marcel Danesi (University of Toronto), Armando Cristinziano and Barbara Toye (North York Board), Izhar Mirza (National Federation of Pakistani Canadians), and Joseph Pizzolante (Etobicoke Board).

On substantive matters, Marcel Danesi, professor of Italian studies, University of Toronto, and James Cummins, professor of education at the Ontario Institute for Studies in Education, made invaluable contributions. The team is especially appreciative of Professor

Danesi's enthusiastic support of the project and his specific suggestions on methodology. He helped the team prepare the first lesson plan (for *Book One*) that was used as a model and has taken a keen interest in the project through the years.

Above all, I must acknowledge the unwavering commitment of the writing team members: Humaira Ansari, the late Firdaus Beg, Rashida Mirza, Zahida Murtaza, and Hamda Saifi. Their multiple roles did not deter them from putting in endless hours writing original stories and preparing creative lesson plans. The second phase was initiated in the beginning of 1993 while the work on the first phase was in its final stages. During the five-year period from 1993 to 1998, the entire group (the writing team, the project director, and the coordinators) spent long days together on weekends and holidays, evaluating and selecting the stories and revising, reviewing, and editing six or seven drafts of each story before field testing. Similarly, the lesson plans were also judiciously reviewed several times before their acceptance.

A special note in memory of Firdaus Beg, an imaginative, compassionate, and conscientious member of the team who fought cancer very courageously during the second phase of the project. In between her frequent visits to the hospital, she made sure to attend the meetings and put her heart and soul into the stories she wrote and the lesson plans she prepared while she was on sick leave from her school. Firdaus lost her valiant fight against cancer on March 17, 2002. The Project team dedicates this set of books to her. She is sorely missed.

Rupert Bottenberg, an artist in Montreal, showed the same commitment to the project as his counterparts in Toronto and Ottawa. Faruq Hassan's translations of the Urdu texts into English helped Rupert overcome the linguistic and cultural barriers, and he impressed the team with his creative and insightful interpretations of the stories through his art. Our special thanks to Rupert for the beautiful and detailed illustrations of the stories, poems, and flashcard vocabulary.

Farhat Ahmad, Faruq Hassan, and Ashfaq Hussain, the coordinators, were the anchors of our writing team. They ably supported the team in every aspect of the project. It was truly well-coordinated teamwork. In addition to my overall responsibility for the Project, Farhat Ahmad and I were intensely engaged in critiquing and editing the original Urdu stories by the team members and the lesson plans for the Teacher's Manual; Ashfaq Hussain and Faruq Hassan reviewed the stories, and typed them for field testing; Faruq Hassan compiled and typed the vocabulary lists; and Ashfaq Hussain spent endless hours in preparing camera-ready copy for McGill-Queen's University Press. Heart-felt thanks to them.

Our deep appreciation is due to those who worked equally hard to impart and preserve an important dimension of children's culture and heritage through sound and music. Jawaid Ahmad Danish and Uzma Danish brought the text of thirty stories to life through their audio recording in narrative style, providing auditory experience to complement the written text. And Nadeem Ali, an accomplished composer and singer, created background music for the

stories and composed original music for the ten poems; he spent endless hours training a children's chorus for the musical versions of some poems, sang some poems solo, and also accompanied the children with sweet rhythms and melodies.

Anwer Saeed Ansari's help is gratefully acknowledged for providing handwritten Urdu sentences and vocabulary for writing-practice exercises for field-testing, and for his help in the preparation of camera-ready copy of *Let's Write Urdu* and *Let's Read Urdu*.

The long list of individuals who shaped and helped produce this work would not be complete without thanking the following: Saqib Mehmood, Institute of Islamic Culture, Lahore, for his assistance in getting the entire manuscript of the Urdu text computer-printed on short notice; Gavin McInnes for scanning the whole project (approximately 600 pages); Nargis Churchill for preparing disks of the camera-ready copy of all volumes except the *Teacher's Manual*; Robert Cameron for doing additional layout; Suroosh Alvi for giving advice on technical matters concerning printing and music recording, and for facilitating access to the artistic and technical talent available in Montreal; and Khadija Mirza for patiently typing several revisions of the *Teacher's Manual* and Introductory sections.

Special thanks as well to the McGill-Queen's University Press and its staff for their keen desire to publish this unusual work. Philip Cercone, executive director, appreciated the significance and intrinsic value of this project all along. This was particularly evident when the Press did not receive the expected publication subsidy from the Department of Multiculturalism in Ottawa and Philip was obliged to raise funds for this publication from various sources. Susanne McAdam, production and design manager, ably steered the course of production, and Joan McGilvray, coordinating editor, edited the English sections of the project and provided helpful suggestions on format and content.

The editor gratefully acknowledges permission to reprint the following copyrighted material: Orca Book Publisher, P.O. Box 5626, Postal Station B, Victoria, BC v8R 6s4, Canada, for "Maxine's Tree," and Shān al-Ḥaqq Ḥaqqī, for his published poem, "Bhā'ī Bhulakkar.

Sajida S. Alvi

CONTRIBUTORS

1. Sajida S. Alvi
   Professor of Indo-Islamic History (medieval and modern periods), Chair in Urdu Language and Culture, Institute of Islamic Studies, McGill University, Montreal

2. Farhat Ahmad
   Retired teacher of English as a second language at the Ministry of Citizenship, Government of Ontario, Toronto

3. Humaira Ansari
   Former teacher at Ottawa Islamic School (primary division); since 1982 has taught Urdu as a Heritage Language at Kehkashan Urdu School, currently under the sponsorship of Carleton Board of Education, Ottawa, Ontario

4. Firdaus Beg
   Teacher of English as a second language, Cherry Hill Public School, Peel Board of Education, Ontario. Former teacher of Urdu as a Heritage Language.

5. Faruq Hassan
   Lecturer in English, Dawson College, Montreal; part-time lecturer in Urdu at the Institute of Islamic Studies, McGill University; Urdu poet; literary critic, and translator of Urdu fiction and poetry into English, and English fiction into Urdu

6. Ashfaq Hussain
   Critic of modern Urdu Literature; writer and Urdu poet, Toronto, Ontario

7. Rashida Mirza
   Teacher of English as a second language and special education, Highgate Public School, York Region District School Board York, Ontario. Former teacher and subject teacher of Urdu Heritage Language programme.

8. Zahida Murtaza

   Grade teacher; teacher of English as a second language, Heritage Park Public School, Toronto District School Board, Toronto, Ontario. Former teacher of Urdu as a Heritage Language.

9. Hamda Saifi

   Programme leader, Parent and Preschooler Programme, Toronto District School Board, Toronto, Ontario. Former teacher of Urdu as a Heritage Language.

10. Rupert Bottenberg

   Commercial illustrator and music editor at the Montreal *Mirror*. Also a published comic artist who organizes the Montreal Comic Jams.

ABOUT THIS BOOK

This course is based on the premises that:

1. Language instruction is effective only if parents take an active role in their child's language acquisition process.
2. A rich language environment, where the child is exposed to a wide range of spoken and written Urdu, provides a solid foundation for language instruction in the classroom.
3. The interest parents show in Urdu in general, and in the Urdu language instruction of their child in particular, is important in motivating the child to learn the language.
4. Parents are urged to speak Urdu with the child as often as possible. The home environment provides an important opportunity for children to see that Urdu can be used to communicate.

The course is designed for two levels, Grade Two and Grade Three. Students are placed in a level based on their facility in the language rather than their chronological age. *Urdu for Children: Stories and Poems* (two volumes) provides material for forty lessons built around topics such as community helpers, science, seasons, ecology, recreation, folktales and fables. These topics were chosen because children at this level are interested in them. Each lesson in the book contains a story or poem accompanied by comprehension questions.

In the classroom setting, the language is presented as a meaningful whole. Each topic is introduced through a story or a poem. The children respond to the selection as a whole while also focusing on the meaning of the text. They experience the text in many ways: by listening to it, repeating it in unison, and reading it from the chart. The children then deal with smaller units, for example, by focusing on word attack skills, sentence structure, and grammar.

Each volume includes two vocabulary lists, each containing the Urdu word, an English transliteration of it, its grammatical category, and its English translation. The lists are alphabetized according to both the Urdu script and the English translation. Each list covers only the vocabulary used in the texts of that volume. Common vocabulary is not repeated in both volumes so if a word is missing in one volume, it can be found in the other one. English meanings of the Urdu words are restricted to their usage in the text. These lists should be

of great help to parents in assisting their children with learning Urdu at home or doing their homework.

The CDs, which contain all forty stories and poems, are also an immensely useful resource for children and for parents who have some familiarity with Urdu.

The methodology used in the course is that of "Activity-Based Learning" and is similar to methods used in courses for teaching language arts in the Canadian public school system. Children are encouraged to acquire language by becoming involved in meaningful activities related to a particular topic. For example, in the lesson on pets, children are asked to draw a picture of their favourite pet and, if possible, bring the pet to class to share with their classmates.

The course assumes that children acquire literacy through exposure to written and oral language, by developing word recognition and through a grasp of the conventions of the written language. Thus in this course, learning to read and write Urdu does not begin with learning the alphabet. The children are, however, encouraged to develop fluency in the basic reading and writing skills.

This structure provides the children with an opportunity to interpret a given topic through creative expression in both the visual arts and the communicative arts, no matter how simple the created art may be. Parents' appreciation of this work provides an added incentive for the child to continue the course.

This course is designed to be used in the classroom but can also be used at home by parents to teach Urdu to their children. It is recommended that parents use the *Teacher's Manual*, where they will find detailed methodology for teaching the materials in the course. *Urdu for Children* includes an interesting collection of stories and poems, which they can read to their children. The children should be encouraged to enhance their reading skills by reading the stories in the *Let's Read Urdu* volumes to themselves, their parents, and their younger siblings. The children also need the *Let's Write Urdu* workbook to learn and practise writing skills.

During the course, parents' co-operation will be solicited in a variety of ways and a positive response is very important. The children will be assigned homework that will require the parent's help. The Urdu teachers may also need their assistance because they often have limited resources for material and support. As well, and most importantly, a positive and encouraging attitude towards school activities provides encouragement and motivation to the child to learn.

Urdu is part of the South Asian Heritage; through the efforts of both teachers and parents children can learn the Urdu language in a way that demonstrates its usefulness and encourages them to be proud of knowing it.

Farhat Ahmad and Rashida Mirza

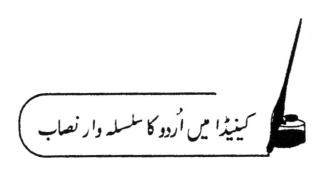

کینیڈا میں اُردو کا سلسلہ وار نصاب

بچّوں کے لیے اُردو کی دُوسری کتاب

آئیں اُردو پڑھیں

(دُوسرا حصّہ)

مدیرِ اعلیٰ

ڈاکٹر ساجدہ علوی

معاونین

فرحت احمد۔ فاروق حسن۔ اشفاق حسین

مجلسِ مصنّفین

حمیرہ انصاری۔ فردوس بیگ۔ رشیدہ مرزا۔ حامدہ سیفی۔ زاہدہ مرتضیٰ

تزئین کار : روپرٹ بوٹنبرگ

فہرستِ مضامین

سہیلی بُوجھ پہیلی

کرن اپنے اَبّو اور اُمّی کے ساتھ ایک دوسرے
شہر میں رہنے کے لیے جا رہی تھی۔ جاتے
وقت کرن نے اپنی دوستوں سے گلے مِل کر
خدا حافِظ کہا ۔ وہ بہت اُداس تھی۔

کرن کے نئے گھر کے قریب ایک پارک تھا۔

پارک میں کچھ لوگ وَرزِش کر رہے تھے۔

کچھ لوگ سائیکلوں پر اِدھر اُدھر گھوم رہے تھے ۔

کرن درختوں کو گِن رہی تھی ۔ ایک درخت پر کرن نے پہیلی لکھی ہوئی دیکھی ۔

ایک قلعے میں نو سو پَریاں

جب دیکھو سَر جوڑے کھڑیاں

جب کھولے قلعے کے پٹ

جی میں آئے کر جاؤں چٹ

وہ پہیلی اِرم نے لِکھی تھی ۔
کِرن اُس سے مِل کر بہت خُوش
ہوئی ۔ اب اُسے نئے شہر میں
ایک اچھی دوست مِل گئی تھی۔

بھائی بُھلکّڑ

دوست ہیں اپنے بھائی بُھلکّڑ

باتیں ساری اُن کی گڑبڑ

راہ چلیں تو رستہ بُھولیں

بس میں جائیں بستہ بُھولیں

غائب   جُوتا   تو   ہے   ٹوپی

غائب   مُوزا   تو   ہے   جُوتا

12

پیالی میں ہے چمچا اُلٹا

پھیر رہے ہیں کنگھا اُلٹا

13

پُراسرار حویلی

نیلوفر اور اس کے ابّا ایک بڑی

سی حویلی میں رہتے تھے - اُن

کے ساتھ جنگل کے بہت سارے

جانور بھی رہتے تھے -

وہاں مگر مچھ اور ہِرن بھی تھے۔

حَویلی کے ایک کونے میں ایک بڑا

15

سا کمرہ تھا جہاں بہت سی کِتابیں
تھیں ۔

نیلوفَر کو کِتابیں پڑھنے کا بہت شوق تھا۔ ایک
دِن اُسے حَویلی کا ایک نقشہ مِلا ۔

وہ نقشے کی مدد سے حَویلی سے باہر نِکلی تو
اُسے دُور ایک جھونپڑی نظر آئی ۔

جھونپڑی میں ایک بُڑھیا بِستر پر لیٹی
تھی ۔

اُس نے بُڑھیا سے باتیں کیں اور اُسے اپنے
بازو کا نِشان بھی دِکھایا ۔ اُسے پتہ چلا کہ
وہی اس کی ماں ہے جِس سے وہ بچپن میں
جُدا ہو گئی تھی ۔

نِیلوفَر اپنی ماں سے مِل کر بہت خُوش ہوئی اور
اُسے اپنے ساتھ حَویلی میں لے آئی جہاں وہ
اپنے ماں باپ کے ساتھ مِل کر خُوشی خُوشی
رہنے لگی ۔

18

ہمدردی

کسی شجر کی تنہا ٹہنی پہ
کوئی اُداس بیٹھا تھا بُلبُل

کہتا تھا کہ رات سر پہ آئی

اُڑنے چگنے میں دِن گذارا

سُن کر بُلبُل کی آہ و زاری

جُگنو کوئی پاس ہی سے بولا

حاضر ہوں مدد کو جان و دل سے

رکیڑا ہوں اگرچہ میں ذرا سا

دوستوں کی ایجاد

خالِد اور نومی نے ایک روبالٹ بنانے کے
بارے میں سوچا لیکن کئی دِن تک وہ یہ فیصلہ
نہ کر سکے کہ اُس سے کیا کام لیں گے۔

پہلے اُنہیں یہ خیال آیا کہ روباٹ سے گھر کی
صَفائی کرائیں مگر گھر گھر میں بہت سے کام تھے ۔
گھر کی صَفائی میں کپڑوں کی دراز ، سنگھار میز ،
کِتابیں ، تَصویریں اور بہت ساری چیزیں تھیں ۔

23

آخِر اُنہوں نے گھاس کاٹنے والا
روباٹ بنانے کا فیصلہ کرلیا ۔

ایک دِن روباٹ تیّار ہو گیا اور اُس نے
گھاس کاٹنی شروع کر دی ۔ اَمّی اور اَبّا اور
پڑوسیوں نے جب روباٹ کو گھاس کاٹتے ہوئے
دیکھا تو وہ سب لوگ وہاں جمع ہو گئے ۔ سب
لوگ خالِد اور نومی کی اِس اِیجاد پر بہت خُوش
تھے ۔

پَت جھڑ

پَت جھڑ آیا پَت جھڑ آیا

رنگ برنگے پتّے لایا

پیڑوں کی پوشاک نئی ہے

ہر اِک ٹہنی جھوم رہی ہے

پتّے   سنہرے   لال   پیلے

پتّے   لرزے   تو   چلی   ہوا

بدلی ہے   کروٹ   نے   موسم

لی ہے   رُخصت   اب   نے   گرمی

کر   کھا   جھونکا   کا   ہوا   خنک

کر   گھبرا   سب   پرندے   بولے

26

پَت جھٹر کی ہے شان نرالی

اپنا جھنڈا اس کی نشانی

سوہنی دھرتی

زمین، چاند اور سُورج آپس میں
بہت اچّھے دوست تھے ۔

جب سُورج آسمان پر چمکتا تو زمین
پر رہنے والے سب لوگ خُوش ہو
جاتے اور اپنے اپنے کام کرتے ۔

پھَل، پھُول، پرندے اور درخت سب
بہت خُوبصورت نظر آتے ۔

ایک دِن سُورج نے سوچا کہ میں
اب بہت بُوڑھا ہوچکا ہوں اس لیے
مجھے آرام کرنا چاہیٔے ۔

جب سُورج نہ نِکلا تو ہرطرف اَندھیرا
پھیل گیا ۔

پرندے گھونسلوں میں دَبکے بیٹھے تھے ۔
ہر کوئی آسمان کی طرف پَریشان

ہو کر دیکھ رہا تھا ۔

آخر چاند نے سُورج کو سمجھایا کہ زمین کو آپ
کی روشنی کی بہت ضرورت ہے ۔ سُورج نے کہا
کہ "بہت اچھا ، اب میں کبھی زمین سے اپنی
روشنی نہیں چھپاؤں گا" ۔ اُس وقت سے آج تک
زمین ، چاند اور سُورج بہت گہرے دوست ہیں ۔

برسات

وہ دیکھو! اُٹھی کالی کالی گھٹا

ہے چاروں طرف چھانے والی گھٹا

گھٹا آن کر مینہ جو برسا گئی

تو بے جان مٹّی میں جان آ گئی

زمیں سبزے سے لہلہانے لگی

کسانوں کی محنت ٹھکانے لگی

جڑی بوٹیاں، پیڑ آئے نِکل

عجب بیل پتّے، عجب پُھول پَھل

صفی میاں کا فارم

صفی میاں کا ہے اِک فارم

شہر سے دُور ہزاروں گام

فارم پہ اُن کے ہے اِک گائے

گھاس جو دن بھر چَرتی جائے

پیٹ   بھرے   گا   جب   گائے   کا

دودھ   ملے   گا   تب   گائے   کا

دودھ   ہے   گائے   کا   اِک   تحفہ

پینے   میں   ہے   بے   حد   اچّھا

دودھ سے ہی نکلے گا مکّھن

بھر لیں گے ہم اُس سے برتن

اس سے کھیر بنائیں گے ہم

اور پنیر بنائیں گے ہم

احمد کا بندر

ایک دن احمد اور اُس کے بھائی
مری میں گھومنے گئے ۔ وہاں اُنہوں
نے ایک دیہاتی آدمی کو دیکھا ۔ وہ
بندر کا بچّہ بیچ رہا تھا ۔ احمد

نے بندر کا وہ بچّہ خرید لیا۔

احمد نے اپنے بندر کا نام چھوٹو رکھا۔ چھوٹو گھر
کے دوسرے جانوروں کو بہت تنگ کرتا تھا۔
کبھی کتّے کے پیچھے بھاگتا تو کبھی بکری کی پیٹھ
پر سواری کرتا۔ سب لوگ اس کی شرارتوں سے

بہت پریشان رہتے تھے ۔

ایک دن احمد کھیلتے کھیلتے ایک گہرے
کھڈے میں گر کر بے ہوش ہو گیا ۔ چھوٹو
گھر والوں کو وہاں لے گیا ۔ ابّو فوراً احمد
کو ہَسپتال لے گئے اور ڈاکٹر نے احمد

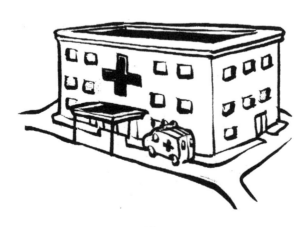

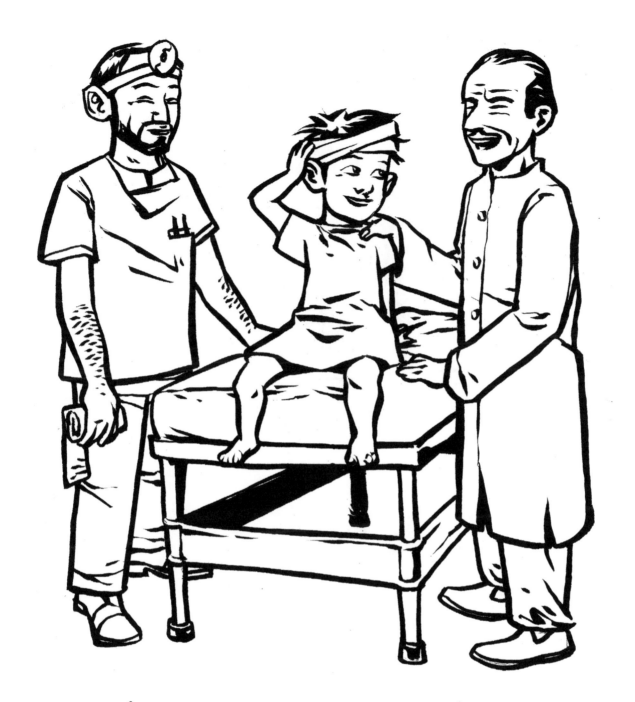

کے سَر کی چوٹ پر دوا لگائی اور
پٹّی باندھ دی ۔

سب لوگ خوُش تھے کہ چھوٹُو نے
احمد کی جان بچائی ۔

خریداری

رحیم اور گریم اپنے والدین کے ساتھ عید کی خریداری کے لیے شاپنگ پلازا میں گئے۔

وہاں دونوں بھائی کِھلونوں کی دوکان
میں کھیلنے لگے۔

اچانک امّی نے دیکھا کہ رحیم اور کریم کہیں غائب ہو گئے ہیں۔

سب لوگ پریشان ہو کر اُنہیں ڈھونڈنے لگے ۔

پلازا کی پولیس نے بھی تلاش کیا
مگر رَحیم اور کَریم کا کہیں پتہ نہ
تھا ۔

دوکان بند ہو چکی تھی ۔ اندر رَحیم
اور کَریم بہت پریشان تھے ۔

اُنہوں نے اندر سے دوکان کا
دَروازہ کھولنے کی کوشش کی تو اَلارم
بجنے لگا ۔

اَلارم کی آواز سُن کر پولیس وہاں
پہنچ گئی - اُنہوں نے رَحیم اور
کَریم کو پیار کیا اور اُن کے گھر
پہنچا دیا-

اُنہیں دیکھ کر سارے گھر والے بہت
خُوش ہو گئے -

مریم کا درخت

مریم اپنی دادی اماں کے ساتھ وینکوور کے جنگلوں میں گھومنے جایا کرتی تھی۔

اس جنگل میں ایک بڑا سا صنوبر
کا درخت تھا جو مَریم کو بہت
پسند تھا۔ اُس درخت کا تنا اِتنا
بڑا تھا کہ مَریم اس کے موکھے
میں بیٹھ جاتی اور کھیلتی ۔

ایک دن مریم اور اس کا چچازاد بھائی پہاڑی
کے اُوپر چڑھے تو اُنہیں برابر والی پہاڑی بالکل
چٹیل نظر آئی ۔ اس چٹیل پہاڑی کو دیکھ کر
مریم بہت اُداس ہو گئی ۔

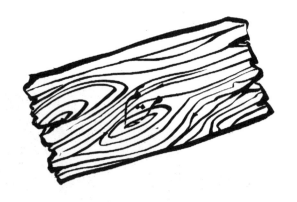

مَریم کے اَبّو نے بتایا کہ درختوں کے کٹ جانے کی وجہ سے یہ پہاڑی چٹیل ہو گئی ہے ۔ مَریم کو فوراً خیال آیا کہ اگر میں اپنے صَنوبر کے درخت پر اپنے نام کی تختی لگا دوں تو پھر اُسے کوئی نہیں کاٹے گا اور یہ جنگل ہمیشہ ہرا بھرا رہے گا ۔

گرمی کی چھٹّیاں

ثناء اور اسد اپنی اَمّی اور اَبّو کے ساتھ کار میں سفر کر رہے تھے۔ رات کافی ہو چکی تھی، وہ لوگ راستہ بھول گئے۔ اچانک اُنہیں ایک گھوڑ سوار نظر آیا۔ اُس کی ٹوپی میں پَر لگے ہوئے تھے اور اُس کی دو چوٹیاں بھی تھیں۔ اُس کے گلے میں ہڈیوں کا ایک ہار بھی تھا۔

اَبّا نے اُس سے کِسی ہوٹل کا راستہ پُوچھا تو
گھوڑ سوار نے کہا کہ یہاں سے دُور دُور تک
کوئی ہوٹل نہیں ہے ۔ میرا نام آرتھر ہے اور
آپ میرے ساتھ آج رات رہ سکتے ہیں ۔

راستے میں وہ ایک میدان سے گزرے جہاں
کینیڈا کے اصلی باشندوں کی سالانہ نمائش لگی
ہوئی تھی ۔

خیمہ میں پہنچ کر آرتھر نے اَسد
اور ثَناء کو اپنے بچّوں سے مِلوایا ۔

اِن بچّوں کے ساتھ ثَناء اور اَسد
نے بہت سے ٹوٹم پول دیکھے ۔

55

وہاں اُنہوں نے خُوبصورت گھوڑے
اور پہاڑی بھینسے بھی دیکھے -

اور آگے پہنچے تو دیکھا کہ کُچھ
لوگ ڈھول بجا بجا کر گانا گا رہے
ہیں -

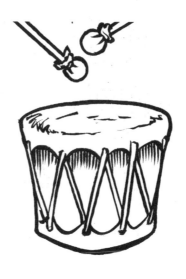

کینیڈا کے اصلی باشندوں سے مل کر
ثناء اور اسد بہت خُوش ہوئے ۔

<h1 style="text-align:center">کشتی کی سیر</h1>

جاوید اور رابرٹ کشتی سے اُترتے ہی
ساحل پر دوڑتے دوڑتے بہت دُور
نِکل گئے ۔

اچانک جاوید ٹھوکر لگنے سے گر پڑا ۔ اُس نے
دیکھا کہ وہ چیز ایک بڑا سا جانور ہے ۔ دونوں
بچّے اُس جانور کو دیکھ کر ڈر گئے ۔

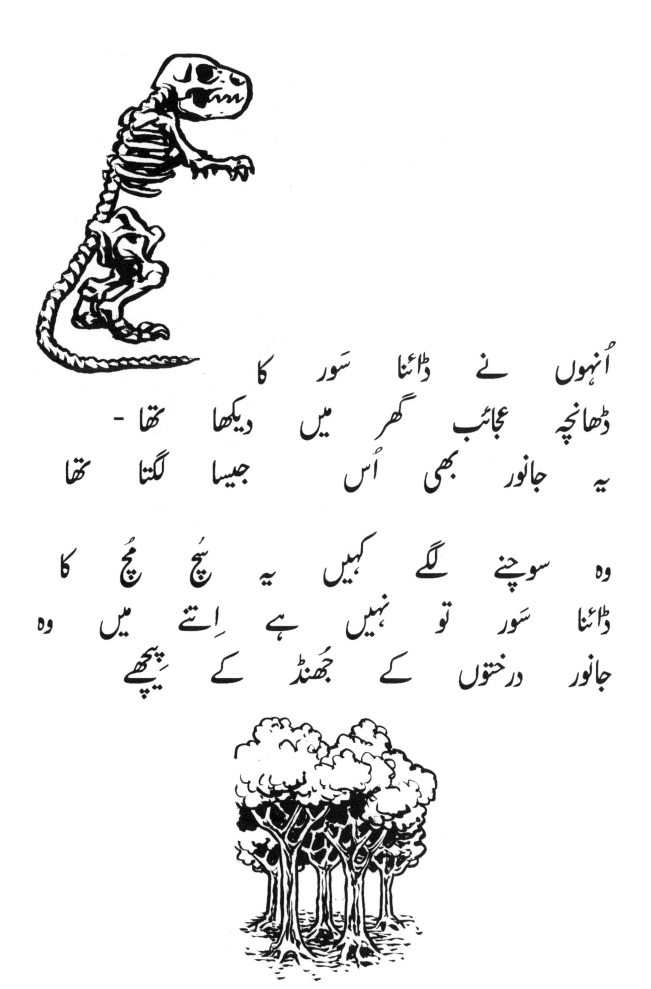

اُنہوں نے ڈائنا سَور کا

ڈھانچہ عجائب گھر میں دیکھا تھا -

یہ جانور بھی اُس جیسا لگتا تھا

وہ سوچنے لگے کہیں یہ سچ مُچ کا

ڈائنا سَور تو نہیں ہے اِتنے میں وہ

جانور درختوں کے جُھنڈ کے پِیچھے

60

کھائی میں غائب ہو گیا ۔

دونوں بچّے اپنے اَبّو اور اَمّی کو بھی وہاں لے
گئے ۔ اَبّو نے کھائی کی طرف دیکھتے ہوئے کہا کہ
یہ ڈائناسور نہیں ہے ، یہ تو اِگوانا ہے جو صرف
پتّے کھاتا ہے ۔

61

برف کا آدمی

آؤ بنائیں برف کا

اِک چھوٹا سا آدمی

ناک ہو اس کی طوطے جیسی ہاتھی جیسے کان

منہ ہو اس کا بندر جیسا لیکن ہو اِنسان

گردن ہو زرافے جیسی بِلّی جیسی مُونچھ

جو بھی اُس کو دیکھے سمجھے یہ ہے اصلی مُونچھ

اس کے سر پر ٹوپی رکھیں نیلی پیلی لال
اُونی مفلر بھی اِک اس کی گردن میں دیں ڈال

آؤ   بنائیں   برف   کا
اِک   چھوٹا   سا   آدمی

64

عامر اور مائیکل سرکس گئے

عامر اور مائیکل سرکس گئے تو
وہ اسٹیج کے پیچھے پہنچ گئے ۔
وہاں خیمے کے سامنے ایک مسخرہ کھڑا
تھا اور دُوسرا مسخرہ قلابازی کھا رہا
تھا ۔

تھوڑی دیر کے بعد سرکس شروع ہو گیا ۔
ایلزبیتھ سفید گھوڑے پر سوار تھی ، وہ سب سے
پہلے خیمے میں داخل ہوئی ۔ اُس کے ہاتھ میں
کینیڈا کا جھنڈا تھا ۔

دو لڑکیاں پِنجرے لیے ہوئے داخل
ہوئیں - اُن پِنجروں میں چِڑیاں تھیں -
ایک لڑکے کے ہاتھوں میں
بڑے بڑے حلقے تھے جس میں سے

کُتّے چھلانگ لگا رہے تھے ۔

اس کے پیچھے پیچھے ایک مَداری بھی آیا ۔

68

سب سے آخر میں دو مَسخرے خیمے
میں داخل ہوئے ۔ وہ دو ہاتھیوں
پر سوار تھے اور اُن کے سر
پر تِکونی ٹوپیاں تھیں۔ اُن کو
دیکھ کر لوگ زور زور سے ہنسنے
لگے ۔

موتیوں کا ہار

کامران سمندر کے کِنارے کھیل رہا تھا ۔ وہ
پانی میں کھیلتے کھیلتے بہت دُور نِکل گیا۔

کامران کو پانی میں رنگ برنگی مچھلیاں نظر آئیں ۔
وہ اُن کے ساتھ ساتھ تَیر رہا تھا کہ اُسے ایک
لڑکی تَیرتی ہوئی نظر آئی ۔ وہ دونوں مچھلیوں کے
ساتھ کھیلنے لگے ۔ لڑکی کا نام سارہ تھا ۔

اچانک کامران کو محسوس ہوا جیسے وہ ڈوب رہا
ہے ۔ سارہ نے کامران کا ہاتھ پکڑ لیا اور اُسے
سہارا دیا ۔ کامران نے دیکھا کہ وہ کوئی عام
لڑکی نہیں ہے بلکہ وہ تو ایک جل پری ہے
اور اُس کے جسم کا نِچلا حِصّہ مچھلی کا ہے ۔

جل پَری کامران کو اپنے محل میں لے گئی ۔
اُس کا پھاٹک سُنہرے رنگ کا تھا ۔ جل پَری
نے محل سے چلتے وقت کامران کو موتیوں کا ہار
دیا ۔

کامران جب ساحِل پر واپس پہنچا تو اُس نے
دیکھا کہ سارہ کا دِیا ہوا موتیوں کا ہار اُس
کے ہاتھ میں نہیں ہے ۔

بلّی کا انوکھا بچّہ

جمیلہ اور اُس کی امّی کو پارک میں بلّی کا
ایک چھوٹا سا بچّہ بلّا جو زخمی تھا ۔ جمیلہ اور
اُس کی امّی اُسے گھر لے گئیں ۔ اُنہوں نے اُس
کی دیکھ بھال کی اور کچھ دِنوں میں وہ ٹھیک ہو
گیا ۔ جمیلہ نے اُس کا نام مانو رکّھا ۔

مانو اکثر رات کو غائب ہو جاتا۔
ایک رات جمیلہ اور اُس کی امّی
نے اُس کا پیچھا کیا۔ اُنہوں نے
دیکھا کہ جھاڑیوں کے آگے ایک
شامیانہ ہے اور مانو اِس طرف چلا
گیا ہے ۔ جمیلہ اور اُس کی
امّی جھاڑیوں کے پیچھے سے اُسے دیکھنے
لگیں ۔

مانو شامیانے میں داخل ہو گیا ۔ وہاں ایک اِسٹیج
بنا ہوا تھا ۔ اُس پر ایک خُوبصورت قالین بِچھا
اور اُس پر ایک گُلدستہ رکھّا تھا ۔

اسٹیج پر مانو آیا اور کُرسی پر بیٹھ
گیا اور بڑے خوب صورت سُر

میں بانسری بجانی شروع کی ۔ اچانک
اُس کی نظر جمیلہ اور اُس کی اَئّ
پر پڑی اور مانو شامیانے سمیت غائب ہو
گیا ۔ اب وہاں کچھ نہ تھا ۔

سادھو کی دُعا

ایک سَادھو ایک درخت کے نیچے دُعا
کر رہا تھا ۔ اُس کے ہاتھ پر
ایک چِڑیا آ کر بیٹھ گئی ۔ وہ
چِڑیا کو اپنے گھر لے آیا ۔

سادھو کے گھر آ کر وہ چڑیا ایک
لڑکی میں تبدیل ہوگئی -

سادھو بیٹی کو پا کر بہت خوش ہوا
اور اُس نے اُس کا نام سونا رکھا۔

82

سادھو کے علاوہ گاؤں کے لوگ بھی
سونا کو بہت چاہتے تھے ۔

جب سادھو اور اس کی بیوی فوت
ہوگئے تو سونا پھر سے چڑیا بن
گئی اور جنگل میں واپس چلی گئی ۔

بی گلہری

بی گلہری آم کے درخت پر بیٹھی تھیں ۔ اُدھر سے بادشاہ کی سواری گزری ۔ اچانک اُن کی سواری پر ایک آم گر پڑا ۔ بادشاہ نے نظر اُٹھا کر جب اُوپر دیکھا تو وہاں بی گلہری بیٹھی ہوئی تھیں ۔

بادشاہ نے بی گلگہری کو اپنے محل میں آنے کی
دعوت دی ۔ بی گلگہری نے محل میں جانے کے
لئے کپڑے خریدے ۔

بادشاہ نے اُن کی سواری کے لیے
ایک ہاتھی بِھجوایا لیکن بی رگلھری نے
اُس پر بیٹھنے سے اِنکار کر دیا کیونکہ
وہ بہت بڑا تھا ۔

جب بادشاہ نے چھوٹا سا نرم بالوں
والا کُتّا بِھجوایا تو وہ خُوشی خُوشی
اُس پر بیٹھ کر بادشاہ کے محل
پہنچ گئیں ۔

محل میں اُن کی خوب دعوت ہوئی

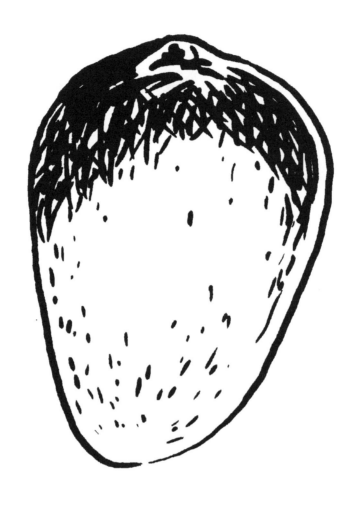

بی گلہری نے مزے مزے کے
آم کھائے ۔ واپسی پر بادشاہ سلامت
نے اُنہیں بہت ساری اشرفیاں بھی
دیں ۔